A Month of Creative Writing Prompts

Written by
Cindy Barden

Editors: Barbara G. Hoffman and Michael Batty

Cover and Interior Design: Good Neighbor Press, Inc.

Illustrator: Chris Nye

FS112135 February Journal Jumpstarts

23740 Hawthorne Boulevard
Torrance, CA 90505-5927

Table of Contents

February

Introduction 1
Best Birthday 2
Groundhog Day 3
Winter Olympics 4
Go for the Gold 5
Never Grow Up 6
I'll Go Down in History 7
Tell the Truth 8
Fun in Groups 9
Very Hairy February 10
Spiderkid 11
Don't Jump to Conclusions 12
Do Over 13
Second Languages 14
Happy Valentine's Day 15
Please Pass the Mustard 16
My Favorite Magazine 17
Driving 18
My Stamp 19
My Heart's Desire 20
My Perfect Bedroom 21
Statue Night 22
Word for the Day 23
Jungle Gym 24
Mardi Gras 25
Cloud Shapes 26
Egg People 27
How Tall? 28
Raindrops 29
Math Machines 30

Introduction

An empty journal is filled with infinite possibilities.

Writing regularly in a journal helps us to develop our imaginations, encourages us to express our thoughts, feelings, and dreams, and provides a way to communicate experiences in words and pictures. Many students feel frustrated when asked to keep a journal. They may not be sure of what to write, or they may be intimidated by a blank sheet of paper. Even professional writers occasionally face "writer's block." The Journal Jumpstarts series provides ideas and suggestions for daily journal entries. Each book contains 29 jumpstarts. You could give each student a photocopy of the same page, or provide a variety of pages and allow students to choose their own topics. You may have students who will be able to sit and write without jumpstarts. At times students may prefer to express their thoughts through drawings or with a combination of drawings and writing. Be encouraging!

Through making regular entries in journals, students become more observant of themselves and the world around them. Journal writing on a regular basis strengthens students' attention spans and abilities to focus. Keeping journals promotes self-esteem because students are doing something for themselves—not for grades or in competition with others. A journal can become an essential friend, a confidante in times of personal crisis.

Encourage students to get into the journal habit by setting aside writing time every day at about the same time, such as first thing in the morning or shortly before lunch. Share their journal time by writing in your own journal. What better way to encourage a good habit than by example!

Note: Assure students that what they write is confidential. Provide a safe, secure place for students to store their journals. Respect their privacy, as you would expect your privacy to be respected—read their journals by invitation only.

Name ______________________ Date ____________

Best Birthday

Write about your best birthday and what happened that made it extra special.

Name ______________________ Date ______________

Groundhog Day

According to legend, if the groundhog sees its shadow on February 2, it means six more weeks of winter. Pretend that something else will happen if another kind of animal sees its shadow. What kind of animal is it? What will happen?

Name ______________________ Date ____________

Winter Olympics

Write about your favorite Winter Olympic sport and tell why you like it.

Name ______________________________ Date ______________

Go for the Gold

Would you like to compete in the Olympics? Why or why not?

Name ______________________ Date ______________

Never Grow Up

Peter Pan wanted to stay a child forever. Write about what it would be like to never grow up. Would you like it? Why or why not?

Name ______________________ Date ______________

I'll Go Down in History

Imagine that 100 years from now people will read about you. Write a paragraph telling what they will read about you.

Name ______________________ Date ____________

Tell the Truth

Some people believe we should always tell the whole truth. Others believe that when the truth can hurt someone else, we should be careful about what we say. What do you believe? Write about what you believe and why you believe it.

Name ______________________ Date ______________

Fun in Groups

Are you a Cub Scout, Brownie, Boy Scout, or Girl Scout? If you are, write about what you like best about scouting. If you aren't, write about another club or organization that you belong to or would like to join.

Name ______________________ Date ______________

Very Hairy February

Many words ends with the sound of "ary," like *berry*, *very*, *cherry*, and *February*. Write some "ary" words. Then use your words to write a short silly poem that rhymes.

Name ____________________ Date ____________

Spiderkid

Imagine getting up in the morning, looking in the mirror, and seeing a huge, hairy spider looking back at you. You've turned into a spider! Write about what you would do if you woke up one day as a spider.

Name ______________________ Date ______________

Don't Jump to Conclusions

Did you ever think something that turned out to be untrue? Write about what you thought and how you found out that it was wrong.

Name ______________________ Date ____________

Do Over

Think about one thing in your life that you would most like to do over again differently. Explain what happened and what you wish that you had done instead.

Name ______________________________ Date ______________

Second Languages

In many foreign countries, children learn at least one language other than their own. Write about whether you think children in the United States who speak only English should learn a foreign language. What language would you most like to learn?

Name ______________________________ Date ______________

Happy Valentine's Day

Think about all the special people in your life, those you love and who love you. Write about one of them and explain why that person is special to you.

Name ______________________________ Date ______________

Please Pass the Mustard

Saying "please" and "thank you" is considered good manners. Chewing with your mouth closed is another example of good manners. Manners are also called "rules of etiquette." Write about three rules of etiquette that you think are important and explain why.

MANNERS

Name ______________________________ Date ______________

My Favorite Magazine

Write about a magazine that you like to read and explain why you like it.

Name ______________________ Date ____________

Driving

Write about what the world would be like if kids were allowed to drive. Would anything be better? Would there be any problems?

Name ____________________ Date ____________

My Stamp

Stamps are often designed to honor important people and events. Create your own stamp to honor somebody or something important to you. Describe your stamp and write about who or what it would it honor and why. Draw your stamp on the back of this page or on a separate sheet of paper.

Name ______________________________ Date ______________

My Heart's Desire

If you could have anything in the whole world, what would you want most? Explain why the thing that you choose is important to you.

Name ______________________________ Date ______________

My Perfect Bedroom

What would your perfect bedroom look like? Describe the color of the walls, pictures or posters on the walls, floor covering, and curtains. On the back of this paper or on a separate sheet, draw a floor plan (a picture of the room the way it would look from above) showing the shape of the room and where your bed and other furniture would be placed.

Name ______________________ Date ______________

Statue Night

If all the statues in a park came to life one night, what would they do? Write a story about what would happen.

Name ______________________ Date ______________

Word for the Day

Open a dictionary to any page. Look through the words on that page until you find one that you don't know. Write the word and its meaning. Then write a story using the word.

Name ______________________ Date ______________

Jungle Gym

Pretend that your school has the biggest and most complex jungle gym in the world. Describe what it looks like, what kinds of things it has on it, and what you would do on it.

Name ______________________________ Date ________________

Mardi Gras

At Mardi Gras celebrations, people dress in fancy costumes. Describe a fancy costume you would like to wear for a party or parade. Explain any special features that it would have.

Name ______________________ Date ____________

Cloud Shapes

Sometimes people watch clouds and pretend that they are something else, like sheep or boats. What's the funniest cloud shape that you have ever seen? Make up a story about your cloud. If you can't remember any funny cloud shapes, think of a shape to use in your story.

Name ______________________ Date ____________

Egg People

What if children were hatched from eggs like birds? Describe what you think the world would be like.

Name ______________________ Date ____________

How Tall?

How tall would you like to be when you are fully grown? Explain why the height that you choose would be good for you.

Name ______________________ Date ______________

Raindrops

Do you like the rain? Tell why or why not.

Name ______________________ Date ______________

Math Machines

Many people depend upon machines like calculators and computers to do basic math like adding, subtracting, dividing, and multiplying. As a result, they forget how to do it themselves. Do you think this might be a problem for you someday? Write about why or why not.